A Wooden Chair

Sarah Ridley

GARETH**STEVENS**
GS
P U B L I S H I N G
A Member of the WRC Media Family of Companies

The author and publishers would like to thank J. K. Bone Ltd, London, and Dylan Pym
for their help with this book.

Please visit our web site at: www.garethstevens.com
For a free color catalog describing Gareth Stevens Publishing's list of high-quality books
and multimedia programs, call 1-800-542-2595 (USA) or 1-800-387-3178 (Canada).
Gareth Stevens Publishing's fax: (414) 332-3567.

Library of Congress Cataloging-in-Publication Data

Ridley, Sarah, 1963-
    A wooden chair / Sarah Ridley.
        p. cm. — (How it's made)
    Includes index.
    ISBN 0-8368-6296-1 (lib. bdg.)
    1. Chairs—Design and construction—Juvenile literature.
    2. Wood—Juvenile literature.   I. Title.
    TS886.5.C45R53   2006
    684.1'3—dc22   2005054072

This North American edition first published in 2006 by
Gareth Stevens Publishing
A Member of the WRC Media Family of Companies
330 West Olive Street, Suite 100
Milwaukee, WI 53212 USA

This U.S. edition copyright © 2006 by Gareth Stevens, Inc.
Original edition copyright © 2005 by Franklin Watts
First published in Great Britain in 2005 by Franklin Watts,
96 Leonard Street, London EC2A 4XD, United Kingdom

Series editor: Sarah Peutrill
Art director: Jonathan Hair
Design: Jemima Lumley
Photography: Andy Crawford

Gareth Stevens editor: Barbara Kiely Miller
Gareth Stevens art direction: Tammy West
Gareth Stevens graphic designer: Charlie Dahl

Picture credits: (t=top, b=bottom, l=left, r=right, c=center)
Argus/Still Pictures: 29c. Digital Vision: back cover t. Mary Evans Picture Library: 10br. Nick Hawkes/Ecoscene: 29t. Hulton-
Deutsch/Corbis: 13t. S. J. Krasemann/Still Pictures: 8b. Robert Maass/Corbis: 28t. Frank Pedrick/Image Works/Topham: 5tr.
Picturepoint/Topham: 30, 31cl. A. Riedmiller/Still Pictures: 4b. Ann Ronan/HIP/Topham: 21b. Ronald Sheridan/Ancient Art &
Architecture Collection: 7t. Paul A. Souders/Corbis: 5bl.

Printed in the United States of America

1 2 3 4 5 6 7 8 9 10 09 08 07 06

Words that appear in the glossary are printed in **boldface**
type the first time they occur in the text.

Contents

The wood used to make a chair comes from a tree.

A chair is a piece of furniture. It has a seat and a strong back to rest against. Some chairs have arms. Some do not have arms. Chairs can be made in many different designs.

This chair is made of beech wood. The seat of the chair has comfortable leather padding. The soft padding on furniture is called **upholstery**.

Beech trees grow tall and straight, producing good wood to make furniture.

Lumberjacks use powerful chain saws to cut down trees.

Making a chair starts when a worker called a lumberjack cuts down a tree. The logs are taken to a sawmill by truck or train or by floating them down a river.

At the sawmill, huge saws cut the logs into long boards, or planks, of lumber. The planks must be dried out. Some wood, such as beech wood, is kilned, which means it is dried in a heated shed.

Sawmills are often built close to forests or woodlands and along rivers.

Why wood?

Wood is easy to cut and shape. Some kinds of wood have unusual patterns or dark colors in them. Other woods are light in color. Some are even red. Wood can be hard or soft. Some woods bend, while others do not. People can make many styles of chairs from the different kinds of wood.

The chairmaker decides what kind of chair to make.

A chairmaker often picks a chair design from a book. The book contains chair designs that have already been drawn. Sometimes, a chairmaker wants to use a new design. A picture of the chair and its measurements are drawn on paper or designed on a computer.

The chairmaker in this book is using beech wood. He buys the wood planks from a lumberyard.

Planks of wood are stacked in a lumber storeroom until they are needed.

In the Past

Except for thrones made for kings, queens, and other important people, the earliest seats were benches and stools. After 1500, furniture makers began to develop styles of chairs, which later became common in most homes. Thousands of years ago, however, ancient Egyptians made chairs similar to the kinds we use today. Some ancient Egyptian chairs survived because they were buried in the tombs of kings and princes.

This throne is more than 3,300 years old. It was found in the tomb of Tutankhamun (ruler of ancient Egypt c.1361–1352 B.C.). Under its decoration, this throne is built like a modern chair.

The chair in this book is being made in a small workshop. Many chairs, however, are made in big factories.

A van or truck delivers the long planks of wood. They are taken into a workshop to be cut up. A team of workers will turn them into a finished chair.

The chairmaker cuts up the planks.

The chairmaker guides the planks under a bandsaw. He cuts them close to the width and the length he wants.

A bandsaw is powered by electricity. Its sharp blade moves up and down through the wood.

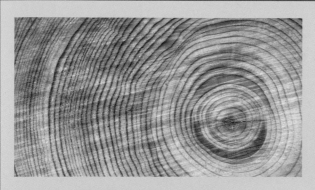

Planks cut from wood at the center of a tree trunk are the strongest.

Why wood?

Wood is very strong because it is made up of many long threads, called fibers. Wood is cut along the grain — along the length of its fibers. Woodworkers learn which kinds of wood are best to use for each job.

The short lengths of wood are taken to a machine called a planer. A planer does two jobs. It shaves off the rough top layer of wood to make the plank smooth. Then the planer slices off layers of wood until the plank is the right thickness for the job.

The chairmaker uses a planer to smooth and thin each plank of wood. The tube behind the planer sucks up the sawdust.

These planks of wood are shown before (*top*) and after (*bottom*) they have been planed. The planed piece is ready for the next step.

The chairmaker cuts the planks to the exact width.

The chairmaker uses an electric circular saw to cut boards to the exact widths he needs.

The sharp blades of a circular saw spin quickly to cut through a board.

In the Past

The surnames, or last names, of our ancestors offer clues to the jobs they did. Sawyer, Turner, Joiner, Carver, and Carpenter are surnames of people whose ancestors probably worked with wood. A sawyer cut wood. A turner shaped it. A joiner made windows, doors, and staircases. A carver decorated wood, and a carpenter made woodwork for houses.

This eleventh-century woodcut shows two carpenters at work.

Next, the chairmaker uses a **template** and a pen to draw the outline of each piece of the chair onto a board. All the pieces of the chair have templates. A template is used to make sure that all the chairs to be made are the same size and shape.

The chairmaker is making more than one chair of this kind. To save time, he draws around a template several times.

back leg template

back support template

These are two of the chair's templates. They are made out of a kind of manufactured wood called plywood, so they will not bend out of shape.

The chairmaker cuts out the legs, seat, and back pieces.

The chairmaker carefully guides the bandsaw's blade along the pen marks. He must cut out all the pieces without mistakes because they have to fit together like a jigsaw puzzle.

Pen marks on the wood outline each piece that must be cut.

The chairmaker needs only a few minutes to cut out each piece.

In the Past

For hundreds of years, except at a few water-powered sawmills, all wood had to be cut with hand saws. Beginning in about 1850, new machines were built to help furniture makers produce decorated furniture much quicker and sell it at lower prices.

This photograph from 1940 shows woodworkers cutting wood using the old saw-pit method. Sawing wood this way required great strength and perfect balance.

Seat pieces are stacked in the workshop.

All the different pieces for the chair's seat, back, and back legs are cut out. The chairmaker uses a fretsaw for very close cutting.

Because the chairmaker is making more than one chair, he has to cut out several of each piece. The pieces are stacked together until they are all cut out.

The chairmaker makes connecting joints.

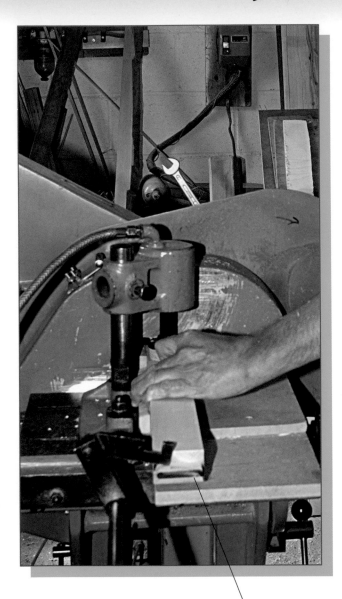

tenon

After a tenon saw has been set up, it cuts tenons automatically. The chairmaker just has to press a button.

Two pieces of wood can be joined with nails, screws, or glue. Chairmakers cut wood into special shapes that fit together tightly to form **joints**. These shapes are called **tenons** and **mortises**.

A tenon saw cuts away the outer sections at the end of a piece of wood, leaving an inner section, called a tenon, sticking out.

Each tenon will fit into a drilled slot called a mortise. A tenon and mortise joint is the strongest way to join two pieces of wood.

Now, the chairmaker makes the mortise slots. First, he puts a leg piece in a mold called a **former**. Pen marks show where the slots should be drilled. He puts the former under the drill, which cuts through the wood.

tenon

former

drill

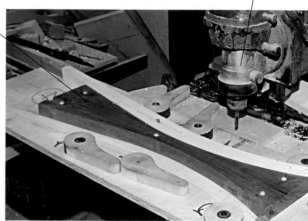

A drill's controls can be set to cut exactly where holes or slots are needed.

mortise

A mortise is cut into one end and the center of each leg piece.

Why wood?

Pieces of wood may be held together with different kinds of joints. To make a joint stronger, a hole can be drilled through the pieces of the joint and a wooden peg or a metal screw can be placed in the hole.

The chairmaker makes the arm and leg pieces.

Each of the chair's arms and front legs are made from one piece of curved wood, using a process called cold-pressing.

First, six thin strips of wood are **laminated**, which means they are glued together in a stack.

To laminate wood for the chair, thin wood strips are coated on both sides with strong glue. Then they are stuck together.

Then, the chairmaker gently bends the stack of wood strips to fit into a mold. He fastens the mold together tightly with clamps.

arm piece

The chairmaker places a mold around the stacked wood to form the chair's front arm and leg.

mold

Why wood?

Wood can be used in many different ways. It can even be bent, either by lamination and cold-pressing or through steam-bending, in which wet wood is bent around a mold, clamped into place, and dried into shape.

Several clamps are used to make sure all the layers of wood stick together evenly.

clamp

After about three hours, the chairmaker takes the laminated wood out of the mold. The wood is now pressed into the correct shape. Next, he will drill holes into the arm end of each piece. The holes will be used for peg joints.

The chairmaker decorates the back pieces.

The back of this chair is made up of four separate pieces. A chairmaker drills a line of holes into the top piece. Then another chairmaker carefully draws squares around the holes. She uses a chisel and hammer to cut out the squares.

Holes are drilled.

top back piece

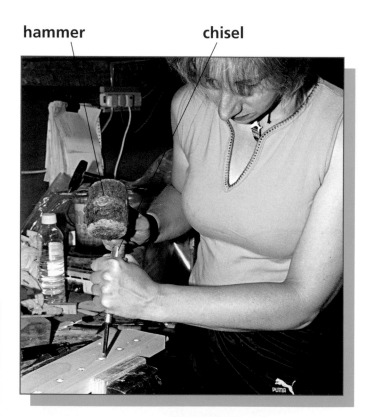

hammer   chisel

Squares are drawn with a pen.

A clamp (*at the bottom of the picture*) holds the wood steady while the chairmaker uses a hammer and chisel to cut out the squares.

Next, she puts glue into the square openings and pushes small squares of walnut wood into them. This kind of decoration is called **inlay**.

A machine called a spindle carves grooves into the pieces that will form the lower part of the back. To make the groves by hand would take much longer.

Small squares of walnut wood are lined up next to the holes they will be placed in.

walnut squares

cutter

This lower back piece is finished. A small tool called a cutter was attached to a spindle to carve the grooves.

Decorating Wood

Besides adding inlays and carvings, wood furniture can be decorated in many other ways. Veneer is a method in which a thin sheet of a beautifully patterned wood is glued onto another kind of wood. Marquetry is similar. It uses thin pieces of different woods as veneer to form a design or a picture.

This beautiful chair from the 1600s has been decorated with both marquetry and carving.

The chairmaker sands the pieces until they are smooth.

A third chairmaker sands the chair pieces to smooth them. For some pieces, he uses a belt sander. He sands other pieces of the chair using a hand sander. Sanding is dusty work so he wears a mask.

The belt sander is a machine that has a revolving belt of sandpaper. The chairmaker uses a sanding pad to press the sandpaper onto the wood.

sanding pad   wood piece   belt of sandpaper

Now the chair pieces are ready to put together. Some slide into place. Others are pegged together.

The chairmaker puts glue in the joints and slides the tenons of the lower back pieces into the mortise on one of the chair's back legs. Then the top piece is set into its mortise. After the second leg is joined at the other side, the back of the chair is complete.

The tenon of a lower back piece slides into the mortise of a back leg.

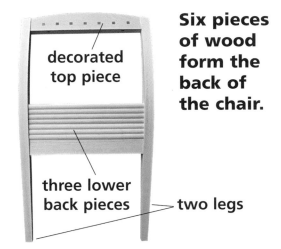

decorated top piece

Six pieces of wood form the back of the chair.

three lower back pieces

two legs

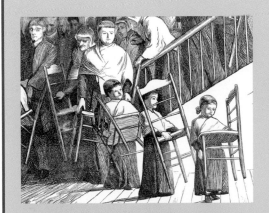

Shakers lived together in communities that shared everything. The design of their ladder-back chairs reflects their simple lives.

In the Past

Certain chair designs are linked to the craftspeople who made them. The Shakers, a religious group that came to the United States from England in the mid-1700s, had a tradition of simple, well-crafted chair designs. These designs are still made today. The Shaker belief that God would notice poor workmanship meant that their chairs were beautifully made.

The chairmaker finishes putting the chair together.

The laminated arm and leg pieces and the seat frame are glued and fitted together.

The chairmaker hammers pegs into the holes at the end of each arm and the holes at the end of each piece of the seat frame.

The front of the chair is put aside until the glue dries.

peg

A peg is forced into each hole. The pegs will help hold the chair together.

Glue goes into the holes first to help the pegs stay in place.

It is finally time to join the front and the back of the chair. The chairmaker puts glue into each hole and pushes the pieces of the chair together.

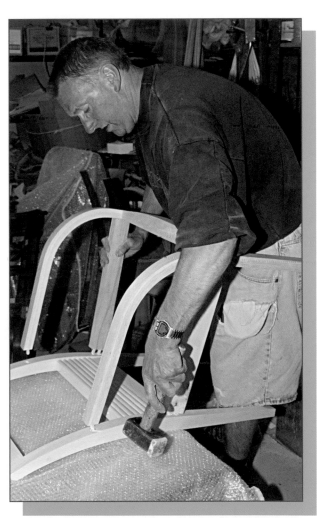

The chairmaker has to work quickly to join the front and back parts of the chair before the glue dries.

Flat-Packed Furniture

Not all chairs are completely put together before they are sold. Some furniture factories make flat-packed furniture. All the pieces of a chair or a table are made with predrilled holes and are boxed up with a bag of metal screws. Because it is built from inexpensive wood, is easy to store and deliver, and the customer (not the factory) has to put it together, flat-packed furniture can save people money.

The chairmaker puts clamps on the chair.

After connecting all the pieces of the chair, the chairmaker adds clamps to hold the pieces together until the glue is dry.

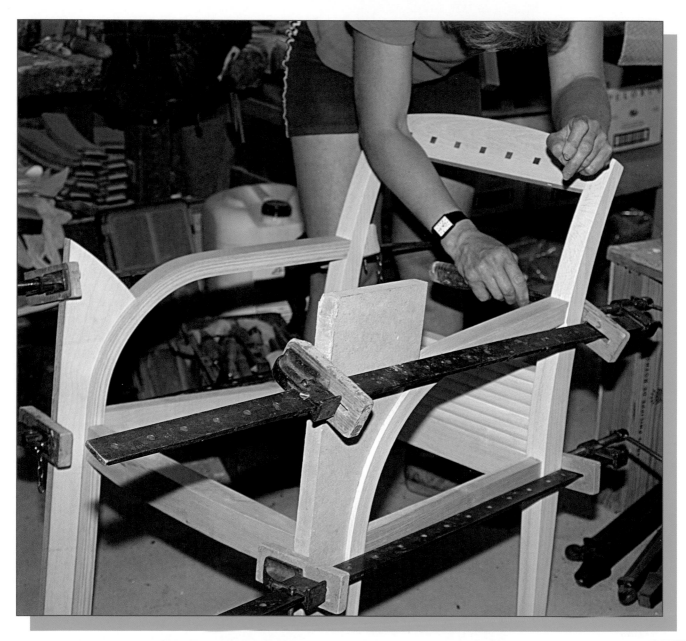

Clamps press all the glued joints of the chair together.

After about five minutes, she takes off the clamps. Then she screws an angled support into each corner of the seat frame to support the seat.

The chairmakers' work is done. The customer will finish the chair by staining, varnishing, or waxing the wood and by adding upholstery, or padding.

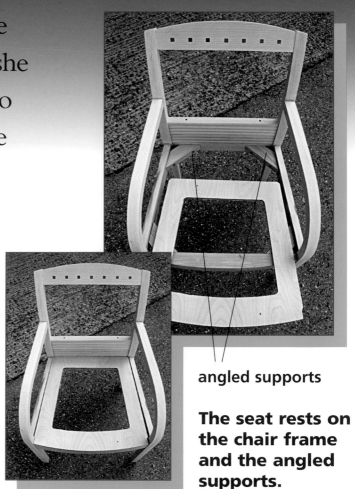

angled supports

The seat rests on the chair frame and the angled supports.

Why wood?

Wood is an adaptable material when it comes to finishing a chair. The same chair can be made to look different in several ways. It can be waxed, stained, varnished, painted, or oiled to make the wood lighter or darker. The seat, and sometimes the back, may be upholstered with fabrics or woven with wicker. If it is taken care of properly, a wood chair can look good for hundreds of years.

This chair was made in the 1800s. Nearly all of it is upholstered.

How a Chair Is Made

In only two days, chairmakers turn planks of raw wood into a finished chair.

1. Planks of beech wood arrive from the lumberyard.

4. A circular saw cuts all the planks to the correct width.

2. The planks are cut with a bandsaw to almost the correct length.

5. A template is used to draw the shape of each piece on the wood.

3. A planer smooths each piece and slices it to the correct thickness.

6. The bandsaw cuts out the pieces along the pen marks.

10. A belt sander makes the pieces smooth.

11. All the pieces are joined.

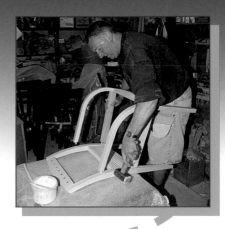

9. The back piece is decorated with inlays of another kind of wood.

12. The chair is ready to be painted or stained and upholstered.

8. The arm and front leg pieces are bent into shape around a mold.

13. The chair is finished.

7. Mortise and tenon joints are cut on some of the pieces of wood.

Other Uses for Wood

People use wood to make many everyday items. A large amount of wood is used to build homes — in window frames, doors, roofs, and floors. Wood is also used to make furniture, such as tables, chairs, beds, and bookcases, that goes inside a house.

Wood can be carved, bent, or hammered together to make musical instruments, sculptures, and toys. It can even be turned into pulp to make paper. How many things can you think of that are made from wood?

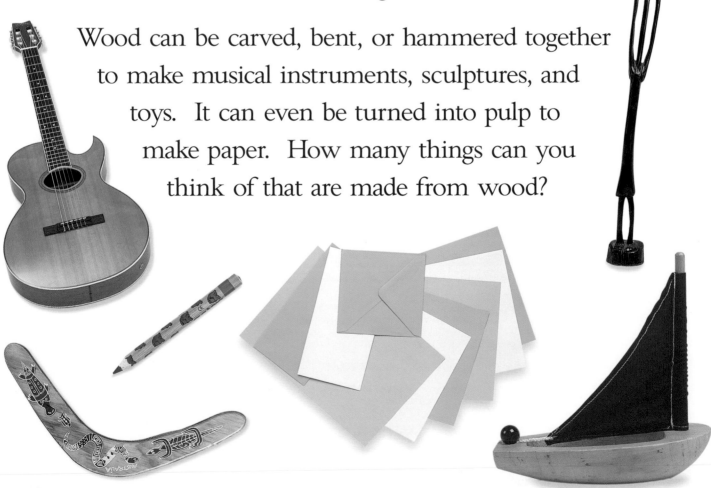

Wood and the Environment

Trees are a renewable resource, which means that, as long as we replant the forests and woodlands we cut down, there will be enough trees and wood for the future.

Sustainable Forestry

The worldwide demand for wood is huge. It has led to many forests being destroyed. Groups around the world are working to encourage good forest management, which is called sustainable **forestry**. Wood from sustainable forests comes with the Forest Stewardship Council (FSC) mark.

Encourage your family to buy wood and wooden furniture that has this mark.

Rotting Away

Unlike plastic or metal, wood will eventually rot away. Old wood can be made into wood chips and used in gardens or on playgrounds.

All Kinds of Chairs

At one time, all chairs were made of wood, but, today, other materials are available. In about 1900, chair designers began to change both the designs of chairs and the materials they were made from.

Now, chairs are made from wood, plastic, leather, metal, fabric, and wicker or various combinations of these materials.

Which of the chairs on these pages do you like best?

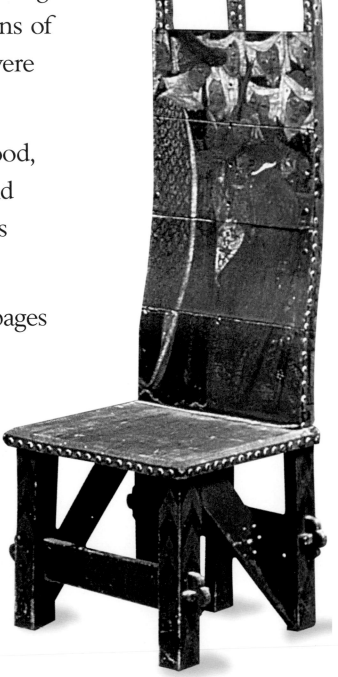

This unusual chair was designed in 1900 by a Spanish architect named Antonio Gaudi. He designed the chair to fit the style of the building it was made for. The chair is made of oak wood and leather.

To break away from the idea that all chairs need four legs, architect Eero Saarinen designed the Tulip Chair in 1957. It has an aluminum base that is coated with plastic and topped with a molded plastic seat.

Many chairs are made of wicker. The frames are usually made of beech wood or metal, then split cane and rattan are woven around the frame to create the chair.

Tubular steel is another modern material used to make chairs.

Glossary

forestry – the science of growing and taking care of forests

former – a mold used to shape wood

inlay – decoration on a flat wood surface using pieces of one or more kinds of wood inserted into another kind of wood, often forming a design or pattern

joints – the places where two parts of something join or fit together

laminated – stuck together in layers, using glue or some other means

mortises – slots or holes in pieces of wood into which tenons on other pieces of wood fit to form joints

template – a pattern or shape used as a guide for cutting out the pieces of something being made

tenons – shaped ends on pieces of wood that fit into mortises, or slots, on other pieces of wood to form joints

upholstery – the soft padding and fabric that covers the solid frames of wood, plastic, or metal furniture

Index